BRICK CITY

PARIS

First published in the United States,
the United Kingdom, and Australia by
Lonely Planet Global Limited
www.lonelyplanetkids.com

2018 2019 2020 2021 / 10 9 8 7 6 5 4 3 2 1

ISBN: 978-1-78701-806-8

This book was conceived, designed, and produced by
The Bright Press, an imprint of The Quarto Group
The Old Brewery
6 Blundell Street
London, N7 9BH
United Kingdom
T(0)20 7700 6700 F(0)20 7700 8066
www.quartoknows.com

Publisher: Mark Searle
Associate Publisher: Emma Bastow
Creative Director: James Evans
Art Director: Katherine Radcliffe
Managing Editor: Isheeta Mustafi
Senior Editor: Caroline Elliker
Project Editors: Alison Morris, Abi Waters
Design: Clare Barber, Lottie Roue, Ginny Zeal

Printed and bound in the UAE

FASCINATING
FACTS
AND
AMAZING
STORIES

BRICK CITY

PARIS

Warren Elsmore

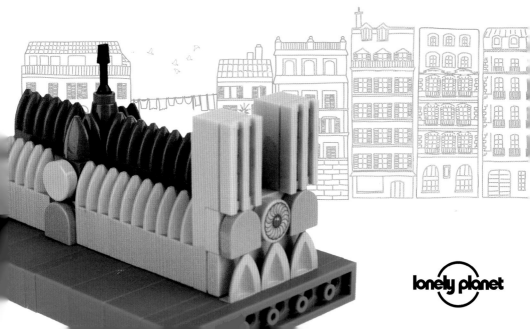

lonely planet

Contents

There are 20 projects in this book to make yourself. Just look out for the brick symbol.

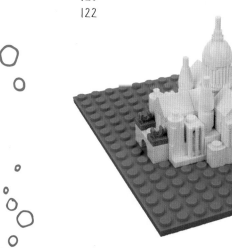

Welcome to Brick City
Paris

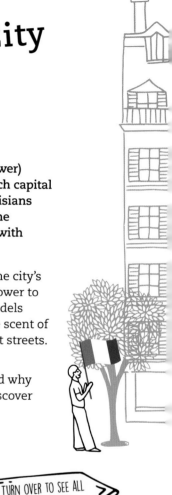

Bonjour! And welcome *mon petit chou* (my little cauliflower) to the most romantic city in the world—Paris! The French capital is elegant, fun, and artistic in equal measure. Here, Parisians fill the sidewalks of charming cafés, monuments line the beautiful boulevards, and art museums rub shoulders with vintage flea markets.

Brick City Paris will take you on a whistle-stop tour of the city's most iconic attractions, from the cloud-piercing Eiffel Tower to cutting-edge fashion. Check out the amazing LEGO® models and scratch your head in wonder while you imagine the scent of freshly baked baguettes and gleaming cobbles of lamplit streets.

Want to know who bakes the president's baguettes? And why street lights are revolutionary symbols? Read on and discover plenty of fun facts along the way.

And you don't have to be a master builder to get involved. Hold the city in the palm of your hand with your very own buildable models, from a buttery croissant to a fluffy poodle. Our expert author will guide you through it all, with tips on LEGO® building and sourcing unusual bricks. The City of Lights awaits. Go ahead and take a stroll!

TURN OVER TO SEE ALL THE BUILDABLES!

Brick Builds

Here's a quick visual guide to all the buildable LEGO® models in this book

STREET LIGHTS
PAGE 109

REMEMBER!
IF YOU SEE ME YOU CAN MAKE IT!

CROISSANT
PAGE 71

PAINT PALETTE
PAGE 90

CYCLIST
PAGE 18

BLACK FOREST
GATEAU
PAGE 67

MACARONS
PAGE 65

TOY BOAT
PAGE 85

PADLOCK
PAGE 29

COFFEE MACHINE
PAGE 77

FLYING MACHINE
PAGE 106

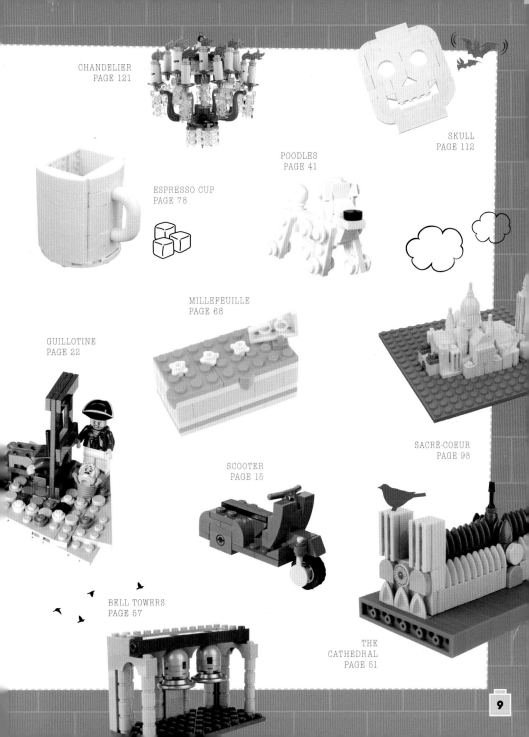

CHANDELIER
PAGE 121

SKULL
PAGE 112

POODLES
PAGE 41

ESPRESSO CUP
PAGE 78

MILLEFEUILLE
PAGE 68

GUILLOTINE
PAGE 22

SACRÉ-COEUR
PAGE 98

SCOOTER
PAGE 15

BELL TOWERS
PAGE 57

THE
CATHEDRAL
PAGE 51

Arc de Triomphe

Work started on the Arc in 1806, but it didn't open until 1836. Unfortunately for Napoleon, France's enemies united against him, and after losing the Battle of Waterloo, he didn't seem so glorious any more.

Work on the arch stopped for 8 years, as Napoleon was ousted to the island of St. Helena. He died there in 1821. He did, however, travel under the arch in his coffin, when he returned as a national hero, in 1840.

72 FEET (22M) DEEP

Underneath is a roll call of military leaders

THE UNKNOWN SOLDIER

Beneath the arch lies the Tomb of the Unknown Soldier. Honoring the 1.3 million French soldiers who lost their lives in WWI, he was laid to rest in 1921, beneath an eternal flame.

164 FEET (50M) HIGH

HOW BIG?

The arch itself is 95 feet (29m) high and 49 feet (15m) wide. Doesn't sound that big? Well, it is big enough for a biplane to have flown through the opening 3 weeks after WWI ended as a tribute to the airmen who had died at war.

148 FEET (45M) WIDE

PLACE CHARLES DE GAULLE

The Arc de Triomphe stands guard in the center of the Place Charles de Gaulle roundabout. Visitors who manage to climb the 284 steps to the viewing platform on top of the arch can see the dozen avenues below and all the crazy horn-honking traffic. The roundabout is well-known as an accident hot spot. It is rumored that some insurance companies won't even cover accidents here!

CLEAN UP

Back in the 1800s, Paris streets were dark, dirty, and smelled of poo! City planner Baron Hausmann—who had been drafted in to help by Napolean III—cleverly introduced drainage, lighting, wider streets, fresh water, and sewers. It took 17 years to clean up and redesign the city.

A FESTIVAL SPECTACULAR

The Christmas lights switch-on happens here at the beginning of December. Crowds gather to watch many of the 588 trees that line the 1.2-mile (1.9-km) long Avenue des Champs-Élysées light up. At the end of December, the streets are closed for New Year's Eve and hundreds of thousands of people gather to see in the New Year.

STREET NAMES

Each of the 12 avenues leading off the roundabout is named after a French military leader.

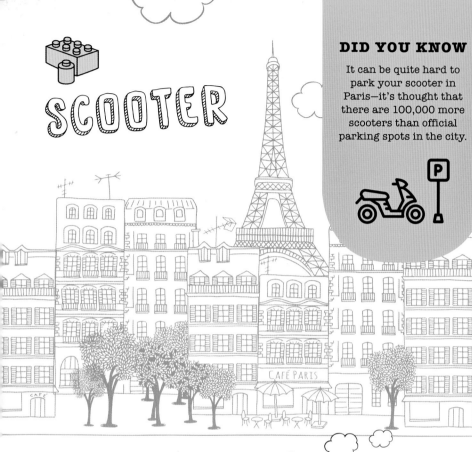

SCOOTER

CAFÉ PARIS

Exploring Paris by scooter is the perfect way to zip around the city—from the hills of Montmartre to the cobbled streets of the Left Bank.

In 2016 the city rolled out an exciting scooter rental app called Cityscoot, which is part of the mayor's plan to reduce traffic and pollution in the capital. On some days the city air is so filled with smog that cars have to be banned for short periods, and public transport is made free to all.

YOU CAN MAKE IT!

Make like a modern Parisian with this stylish mini scooter model. Now you just need to find a figure who is ice-cool enough to drive it!

BRICKS NEEDED

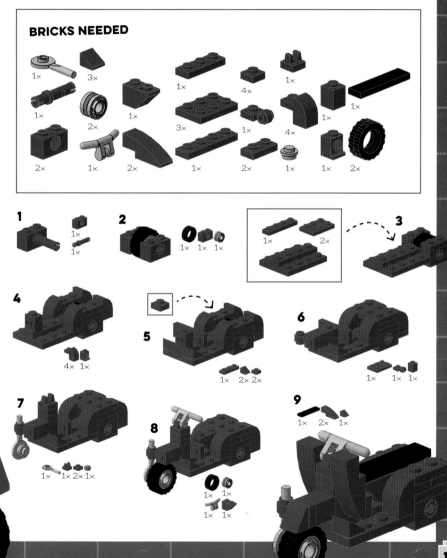

Tour de France

The Tour de France cycle race began as a publicity stunt by a journalist. The race route changes each year and can even start off in a completely different country!

Winners in different tour categories get given different jerseys. Yellow goes to the rider with the shortest total time and green for the most points.

TOUR DE FRANCE IN NUMBERS

124,000 is the approximate number of calories the average cyclist will burn during the whole race.

28,000 is the number of road signs used to mark the route and give warnings to the cyclists.

10-12 million spectators line the route, making it the largest sporting event ever.

THE YOUNGEST RIDER TO EVER WIN THE TOUR DE FRANCE WAS 19-YEAR-OLD HENRI COMET WHEN HE WON IN 1904.

LOOP THE LOOP

The race is often called *La Grande Boucle*, which means "the big loop." This refers to the route that the cyclists take around France.

Cyclist

BRICKS NEEDED

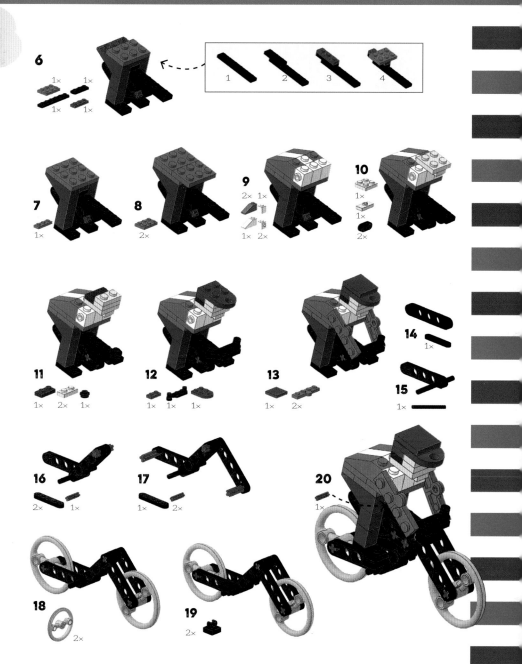

Place de la Concorde

Back in the 18th century, French royals were having a bit too much fun splashing the country's money about. Meanwhile, ordinary French folk could barely afford to feed themselves. The peasants decided to start a revolution, and it wasn't long before heads began to roll...

King Louis was tried for crimes against the people, found guilty, and executed in 1793. Twelve hundred horsemen accompanied his carriage to Place de la Concorde, where the sharp blade of the guillotine whooshed down from its tall wooden frame and sliced off his head. A guard held up the head for the crowd to see and cheers rang out. There would be no more greedy royals! Today, this is the largest square in Paris. A tall pink obelisk marks the spot where the guillotine once stood.

THE CONCIERGERIE

Thousands of enemies of the Revolution were thrown in jail here during the "Reign of Terror," before being put on trial and executed in the Place de la Concorde. Two thousand prisoners were imprisoned at the Conciergerie.

FIT FOR A QUEEN

Many died from the terrible conditions in the Conciergerie prison before they even reached the guillotine. The king's wife, Marie Antoinette, was given special treatment—Revolution leaders didn't want her to die before they chopped off her head in public!

Place de la Concorde—the site of many beheadings

THE FIRST TIME

One of the first heads to roll (sawn off by the angry mob) was Bernard-René Jourdan, Governor of the Bastille prison.

TURN OVER TO MAKE

Guillotine

Guillotine toys were popular in revolutionary Paris; children chopped the heads off dolls and even live rats. Yuck!

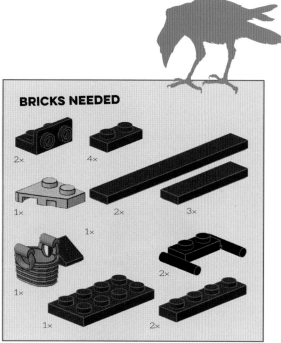

BRICKS NEEDED

2× 4×

1× 2× 3×

1×

1× 2×

1× 2×

1  2×

2  1×

3  1×

4  2×

5  2×

6

2× 1×

7

1×

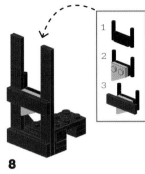

1
2
3

8

1× 1× 1×

9

1×

12

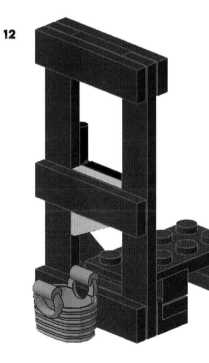

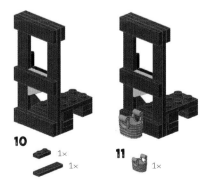

10

1×
1×

11

1×

PONT NEUF

In the 17th century, Pont Neuf was a design sensation. Its name means "new bridge," but at over 400 years old, it's now the oldest bridge in Paris! Back in 1607, though, it was thoroughly modern. Who'd ever heard of a bridge with no houses on it? Or one built of stone, not wood... and wider than any city street?

Everything happened on the bridge: theatre shows, markets, fights. It was also the scene of some of the world's earliest traffic jams. The bridge was a meeting place for rich and poor, but it was said that if you stepped on one side in your fanciest clothes, you'd step off the other wearing nothing!

WRAP IT UP

In 1985, US artists Christo and Jean-Claude used 450,000sq ft (41,800sq miles) of fabric, 8 miles (13km) of rope, and 12.1 tons (11 tonnes) of steel chains to wrap up the bridge!

PAVING THE WAY

Horses carried passengers across the bridge in fancy new carriages. Meanwhile, "people of foot" (the word "pedestrian" hadn't been invented yet) had their own bit of the bridge to walk on as Pont Neuf had one of the world's first sidewalks.

A ROYAL OPENING

In the days when many people paid a boatman to take them from one side of the Seine to the other, the building of a new bridge was a pretty exciting event. And there couldn't be a grander way to open it than for the king, Henry IV, to ride across it on his white stallion.

381 HEADS GAZE OUT FROM THE SIDES OF PONT NEUF, AND THEY ALL HAVE WEIRD AND WONDERFUL EXPRESSIONS TO SCARE OFF EVIL SPIRITS.

LIFE'S A BEACH

For four weeks in July and August, 5,511 tons (5,000 tonnes) of fine golden sand are dumped onto the banks of the River Seine. Parisians play volleyball, lick ice cream, lounge beneath palm trees on oversized deckchairs, and cool off under de-misters.

THE BRIDGE IN NUMBERS

12 arches, with Île de la Cité in the middle

761 feet (232m) long

72 feet (22m) wide

Pont des Arts

What could be more romantic than visiting Paris's Pont des Arts with your true love, clipping a padlock to the bridge and tossing the key into the Seine River to suggest that your love will last forever? One couple did this in 2008 and eight years later, a million others had followed their lead. After a railing collapsed, workers arrived with bolt cutters to remove 700,000 "love locks," and replaced them with shatter-resistant glass panels.

The "love locks" of Pont des Arts

Some couples have switched mediums and have vandalized the glass with indelible pens. Couples looking to express their love will find no shortage of less damaging alternatives in this romantic city, though. Flowers, perhaps?

Padlock

YOU CAN MAKE IT!

Parisians who are worried about covering up the city's most beautiful locations have started an online petition called No Love Locks. Their motto is "Free your love, save our bridges." This padlock is too cute to ruffle feathers.

BRICKS NEEDED

2× 2× 2× 1× 1× 1× 1× 2× 2× 1× 1× 1× 4× 2× 2× 2× 2× 1× 2×

1

2 2×

3 1×

4 1× 1×

5 1× 2× 1×

6 2× 2×

7 4×

8 1×

9 2× 2×

10 2× 1×

11 1× 2×

12 2×

13 2× 1×

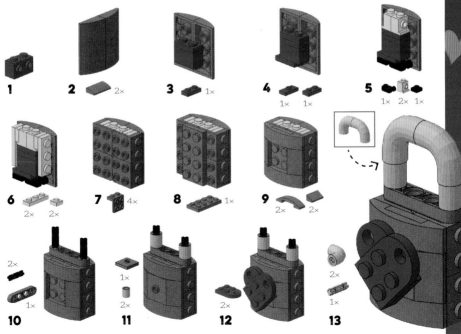

Love is in the Air

Just the thought of beautiful Paris makes some people come over all romantic, and there are certainly some truly romantic places in the city. One enthusiastic visitor even married the Eiffel Tower!

The French language alone makes some people come over all gooey. It is lovely to listen to and French is actually known as a "romance language" because it developed from the Latin that the Romans used to speak. The French for I love you is *je t'aime*.

The *Je t'aime* wall

In a corner of Montmartre, what looks like a huge blackboard is actually a wall of handpainted "I love yous"— and a work of art! Frédéric Baron and Claire Kito (they're not a couple) created the wall after Frédéric discovered he found it easier to say "I love you" in a foreign language rather than in his native language, French.

Scribbles of love on the *Je t'aime* wall

The Kiss

It was unveiled in 1901 and immediately people saw it as a symbol of romantic love. But the lovers are characters from a story and it turns out the girl already had a husband. The husband went on to kill the couple, who were doomed to walk through Hell.

THE KISS IS ONE OF SCULPTOR AUGUSTE RODIN'S MOST FAMOUS WORKS.

PARIS FASHION WEEK

Haute couture literally means "high sewing." It describes the sort of fashion found on the catwalk, not the ordinary stuff worn on the street. The Paris fashion haute-couture shows happen in advance of each season, so the spring/summer collections are in late January and the autumn/winter shows in early July, so that everyone can shop in advance. Most *couturiers* (designers of made-to-measure clothes) also present a *prêt-à-porter* (ready-to-wear) collection, too.

Shows are exclusive affairs, not open to the general public. The front row is the place to be seen, full of celebrities, fashion editors, and bloggers, and everyone dresses their best to make sure that they are noticed. Tourists can check out the afternoon fashion show at the Galeries Lafayette department store instead.

Haute couture in full swing

THE APPROVAL PROCESS

You must be approved by the Chamber of Syndicale, the governing body of fashion in Paris, if you are to be considered an haute-couture designer.

CATWALK IN NUMBERS

2,500 people viewed Christian Dior's new collections in the 1950s.

Shows lasted **2.5** hours, with up to **200** outfits.

CITÉ DE LA MODE ET DU DESIGN

Known as "the Docks" for short and looking like a giant green crocodile, this refurbished warehouse stands out from the crowd, just like some of the fashions that parade the catwalk inside. The building houses the French Fashion Institute (Institut Français de la Mode), with shows and exhibitions held here. In 2012, the Paris Ethical Fashion Show took place here and featured dresses made from recycled film and old bottle tops!

MODELS NEEDED

In the 1500s, fashion designers used to show off their new designs on miniature dolls. The first models were used in 1853.

OUT-THERE FASHION

Haute-couture clothes are known for being totally wild and wonderful, crafted from luxurious fabric, feathers, and Swarovski crystals. World-famous "wild child" French designer Jean Paul Gaultier is known for putting men in punky skirts and Madonna in a conical bra.

Gaultier designs on the catwalk

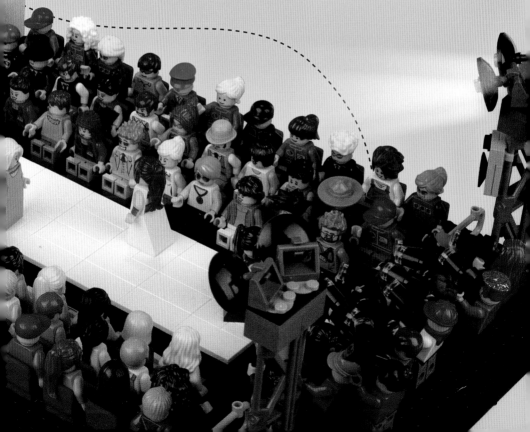

SHOPPING IN PARIS

When it comes to shopping, Paris has it all: broad boulevards lined with flagship fashion houses and international labels, famous *grands magasins* (department stores), and fabulous markets. The real charm of Parisian shopping lies in strolling the backstreets, where tiny specialty shops and quirky boutiques sell everything from strawberry-scented wellington boots to heavenly fragranced candles.

Three Parisian streets form fashion's Golden Triangle. Here shoppers can drool over the latest designs from the finest fashion houses. Most people can't afford to buy, but they're not called window shoppers. In France, it's *lèche-vitrines*—window lickers.

AN UNUSUAL GIFT

Paris is famous for its shopping, but not many would expect to buy a bird of prey or tiger dressed in human clothing here! Shoppers can do just this at taxidermy store Deyrolle. The ancient art of stuffing dead animals has been practiced here since 1831.

IT'S A WRAP

Ask for *un paquet cadeau*—this is free (and very beautiful) gift wrapping, offered by most shops.

SHOPPING ETIQUETTE

People just browsing tell staff *Je regarde* (I'm just looking).

Bargaining is only really acceptable at flea markets.

In exclusive shops, shopkeepers don't appreciate people touching their goods.

Perfume

In the 15th century, washing went right out of fashion—it was thought to be dangerous and unhealthy! New perfumes were developed to cover up the stench.

Ingredients were grown in the south of France and sold in Paris, which quickly became the perfume capital of the world. This history is celebrated in Fragonard's *Musée du Parfum* (Perfume Museum), which has 5,000 years of fragrant tales!

ICONIC SCENT

Chanel No.5 is one of the most iconic fragrances of all time. It was created by Ernest Beaux in 1921 for Coco Chanel.

Copper vats for making perfume

PERFUME IS TRADITIONALLY MADE IN COPPER DISTILLERY VATS, USING THE PROCESSES OF DISTILLING TO CONCENTRATE A FLOWER'S FRAGRANCE. THE MOST EXPENSIVE ARE STORED IN HAND-PAINTED BOTTLES.

BULY 1803

This is possibly one of Paris's most fragrant shops. It was first opened over 200 years ago by Jean-Vincent Bully, whose signature perfume, Vinaigre de Bully (Bully vinegar!), was a 19th-century sensation. Inside the shop, it's like stepping back in time. For a boar-bristle hairbrush, some emu oil, or an actual bottle of the famous scent, look no further. And with no added ingredients, everything in here is nice and natural.

POODLES

REAL POODLES COME IN FOUR DIFFERENT SIZES. THIS MODEL IS SERIOUSLY ADORABLE AND IT DOESN'T REQUIRE ANY GROOMING!

Paris is synonymous with poodles. These dogs were originally bred for hunting ducks, but nowadays they are more often found holding their heads high as they swish their smartly groomed tails on the cobbled city streets.

Le Cimetière des Chiens

Strictly speaking, *Le Cimetière des Chiens* is a cemetery for dogs, but other pets—cats, horses, sheep, rabbits, fish, and even a monkey—are buried here, too. Barry the trench dog is the cemetery's biggest hero, though. He's said to have dragged 41 wounded people from a battlefield, and then keeled over from exhaustion!

Poodles are renowned for being clever

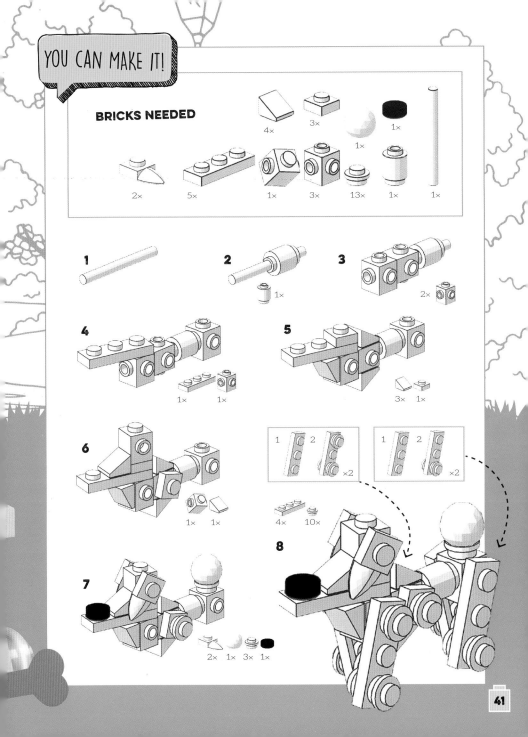

YOU CAN MAKE IT!

BRICKS NEEDED

4×   3×   1×   1×

2×   5×   1×   3×   13×   1×   1×

1

2   1×

3   2×

4   1×   1×

5   3×   1×

6   1×   1×

1   2   ×2

1   2   ×2

4×   10×

7   2×   1×   3×   1×

8

EIFFEL TOWER

The iconic Eiffel Tower was built for the World Fair in 1889, 100 years after the French Revolution. It was erected as a temporary structure, but has towered over the city ever since. The "metal asparagus" was the tallest structure in the world for 41 years—it's still the tallest in Paris. Queues form daily to climb the 1,665 steps.

Today, its outline is the most famous shape in the city, but before it was built, many were furious at the very idea of it. A group of important artists wrote a stiff letter in protest. By 1889, some of them had changed their minds; one composer even wrote a piece of music inspired by the tower.

ON ITS 100TH BIRTHDAY, TIGHTROPE WALKER PHILIPPE PETIT STEPPED ALONG A VERY THIN WIRE FROM THE PALAIS DE CHAILLOT TO THE TOWER'S SECOND LEVEL.

THE TOWER IN NUMBERS

1,063 feet (324m) high

5,300 drawings and designs produced by the engineers and designers working on the tower

20,000 lights twinkle on the tower at night for 5 minutes every hour, on the hour

IN 2015, THE TOWER HOSTED ITS FIRST EVER RACE. THE WINNER REACHED THE TOP IN 7 MINUTES 50 SECONDS!

The tower is made of lacy wrought iron

SAVED BY SCIENCE

From the start, the tower's designer, Gustave Eiffel, pointed out its importance to science. He built the tower from iron, because it was resistant but not too heavy.

Fake fashion

Tourists might be tempted by lookalike Louis Vuitton handbags or Gucci sunglasses being sold by street vendors near the Eiffel Tower—at a fraction of the cost of the real thing. But this street trade is illegal. Just buying a fake bag is a crime with big fines.

EIFFEL BUILT A LABORATORY INSIDE, WITH EQUIPMENT FOR OBSERVING WEATHER AND THE STARS. WHEN IT WAS SUPPOSED TO COME DOWN, IT WAS SAVED BECAUSE OF A NEW-FANGLED RADIO-TELEGRAPH STATION AT THE VERY TOP.

PAINT JOB

Every seven years, a team of 25 painters sets out to repaint the whole structure. The job takes around 18 months, and sometimes involves a complete change of color.

THE TWINKLING TOWER

From 1925 until 1936, 250,000 colored lamps on the tower spelled out "Citroen" in a giant advert for Citroen cars. In 1937, architect André Granet hung a gigantic chandelier with 6.2 miles (10km) of colored fluorescent tubes underneath the tower. And, in 1978, 30,000 bulbs turned the tower into a Christmas tree of light.

L'AQUARIUM DE PARIS

VISIT THE COLORFUL AQUARIUM TO WALK THROUGH THE SHARK TUNNEL.

The Aquarium de Paris—near the Eiffel Tower—opened all the way back in 1867. It was one of the first aquariums built anywhere in the world and is still very popular today.

Paris is spoilt for good aquariums. The Aquarium Tropical is located in the basement of the beautiful *Palais de la Porte Dorée* (Palace of the Golden Gate). It's home to more than 15,000 marine creatures—including a gang of toothy crocodiles—all of them bobbing around in 39,626 gallons (150,000 liters) of water.

FISHING FELINES

Speaking of fish, the narrowest street in Paris also has one of the strangest names—Street of the Fishing Cat (Rue du Chat Qui Pêche)! It's named after the story of an alchemist's black cat that used to walk down the lane to reach the River Seine, where it always caught a fish. Some students killed the cat, but it's said to have later reappeared and carried on fishing. Spooky, huh?!

SHARK SLEEPOVER

In 2016, the aquarium organized a competition to attract publicity. The lucky winners were given the chance to sleep over in the shark tank, submerged in a glass room. It's hard to imagine that they got much sleep!

NOTRE-DAME
DE PARIS

When Victor Hugo wrote his classic novel—*The Hunchback of Notre-Dame*—about a hunchback called Quasimodo, he never dreamed that, more than 100 years later, it would be well-known around the world.

The story takes place around Notre-Dame Cathedral in the Middle Ages. Quasimodo lives in the bell tower, cut off from the world. His face is disfigured and he's deaf from the ringing bells. A gypsy girl, called Esmeralda, shows him kindness and he falls in love with her. When Esmeralda is sentenced to death, Quasimodo saves her by swinging down on one of the bell ropes and sweeping her to safety. The book's French title is *Notre-Dame de Paris,* and in fact the cathedral, not the hunchback, was Hugo's real hero. He wanted to make people appreciate Notre-Dame's gothic architecture, and he certainly succeeded!

BIRTHDAY PRESENT

On Hugo's 80th birthday, a Paris street was named after him. Now there's a street in his name in many towns across France!

Who was Hugo?

Victor Hugo was born in 1802. He's well known in France as a poet, playwright, and author of many novels—he wrote 100 lines of poetry and 20 lines of prose every morning! However, it's his two novels, *The Hunchback of Notre-Dame* and *Les Misérables* (also set in Paris) that made him famous abroad. Hugo was one of the first authors to include characters from all walks of life in his books—from kings to peasants.

TURN OVER TO MAKE

THE CATHEDRAL

A Gothic masterpiece, this Notre-Dame has amazing "rose" windows and huge bell towers. This cute mini cathedral is a lot quicker to build than the real thing!

The cathedral is famous for its striking architecture

WHO'S THE BOSS?

In 1804, Napoleon decided it was time he was crowned Emperor. He booked Notre-Dame and the ceremony lasted more than five hours!

BRICKS NEEDED

1×
2×
2×
2×
3×
2×
2×
1×
4×
1×
2×
1×
1×
2×
2×
1×
1×
33×
1×
21×
2×
5×
1×
2×
2×
6×
1×
6×
4×
1×
1×

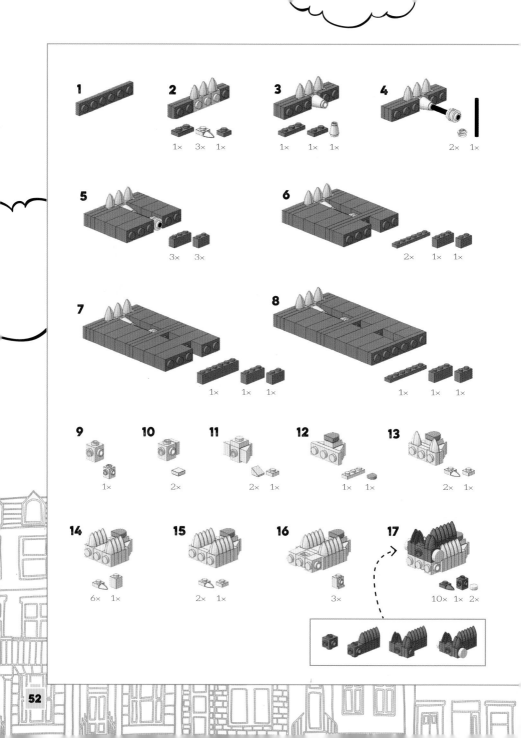

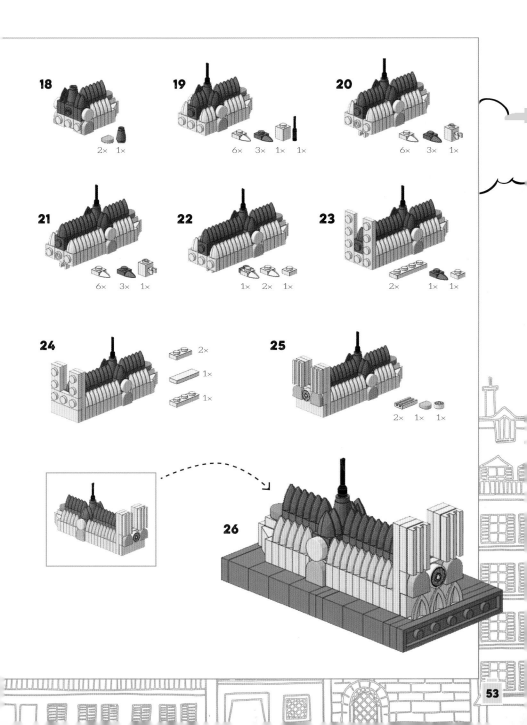

18   2× 1×

19   6× 3× 1× 1×

20   6× 3× 1×

21   6× 3× 1×

22   1× 2× 1×

23   2× 1× 1×

24   2× 1× 1×

25   2× 1× 1×

26

Stained Glass

The cathedral has 176 amazing stained-glass windows, all dating back to medieval times. They miraculously survived a fire in 1194 and are famous for their deep colors, most commonly known as "Chartres blue."

Notre-Dame's size is difficult to miss. The inside is 417 feet (127m) long and it has room for 6,000 worshippers, so it's not hard to find a seat. It is famous for its "flying buttresses." No, they're not anything to do with butts! They are fancy arches that help to hold the whole cathedral up.

Close-up of a "rose" window

WHAT ARE THEY ABOUT?

Some of the stained glass windows in Notre-Dame depict the legend of Saint Genevieve, the patron saint of Paris.

THE THREE CIRCULAR "ROSE" WINDOWS CAST A BEAUTIFUL LIGHT. THE BIGGEST "ROSE" IS 33 FEET (10M) WIDE. IT SITS ABOVE A MASSIVE ORGAN WITH 7,800 PIPES, FIVE 56-KEY KEYBOARDS, AND A 32-KEY PEDALBOARD.

Bell Towers

A constant queue marks the entrance to the cathedral's bell towers. From the rooftop there's a spectacular view over Paris. In the South Tower hangs Emmanuel, the cathedral's original 14-ton (13-tonne) bell. During World War II, when the Île de la Cité was retaken by French, Allied, and Resistance troops, the ringing of the Emmanuel announced the approach of liberation. Its pure sound comes from the precious gems and jewels women threw into the pot when it was recast in 1631.

In 2013, nine new bells were installed to celebrate Notre-Dame's 850th birthday (the old bells sounded awful). Each new bell has a name, just like the very first ones, which were melted down for cannons during the French Revolution.

Did you know that the official name for a bell-ringer is a campanologist? These model bells don't ring but they do look good enough for Quasimodo himself to swing on!

BRICKS NEEDED

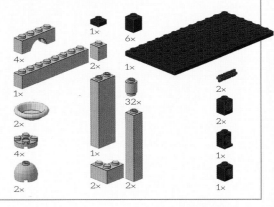

4× 1× 6×
1× 2× 1×
2× 32× 2×
4× 2×
2× 1× 1×
2× 2× 1×

1 32×

2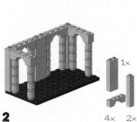

1×
4× 2×

3

2×
1× 2×

1 2 3 4

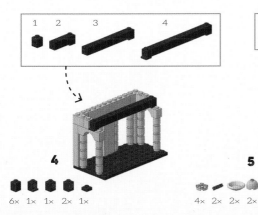

4

6× 1× 1× 2× 1×

1 2 3 4 ×2

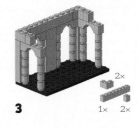

5

4× 2× 2× 2×

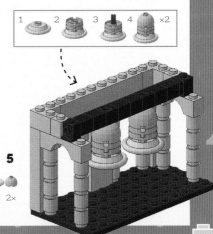

ROOFTOPS

Paris's historic apartments and boulevards are seriously beautiful, with ornate balconies, picturesque shutters, limestone walls, and zinc roofs. Space has always been at a premium and even Haussmann chose to build up, up, up during his renovations (see page 12).

Nowadays, the majority of people in the center of the city live in apartments. Lots of them have "mansard" roofs with distinctive double slopes, attractive port-hole windows, and beautiful balconies—the perfect spot for a morning croissant! Around the 1830s the top floors housed tiny rooms for maids while their wealthy employers lived on the lower floors.

5 BEST ROOFTOP VIEWS IN PARIS

1. Montparnasse Tower
2. La Grande Arch in La Défense
3. The Pompidou Centre
4. The towers of Notre-Dame
5. Tour St Jacques

ENJOY VIEWS FOR MILES ACROSS PARIS ROOFTOPS.

The city rooftops look like a silver carpet

Stand at any Paris viewpoint and the city rolls out in front of your eyes like a carpet of silver. Years of craftsmanship have kept the rooftops in good shape. Paris's roofers applied to UNESCO in 2015 to get the roofs listed for special World Heritage status and protection, but they won't know the result until 2019.

RIVER HERITAGE

The banks of the River Seine are the only UNESCO World Heritage Site in the city centre, even though UNESCO is actually based in Paris!

PÂTISSERIES

Paris cooks up some of the finest cakes and pastries on this planet! Pâtisseries (pastry shops) are similar to bakeries but are generally a notch up on the sophistication scale.

Although they sell different varieties of cake, each one is known for a different specialty. Local children grow up on tartes from Gérard Mulot and chocolate-cream éclairs from L'Éclair de Génie.

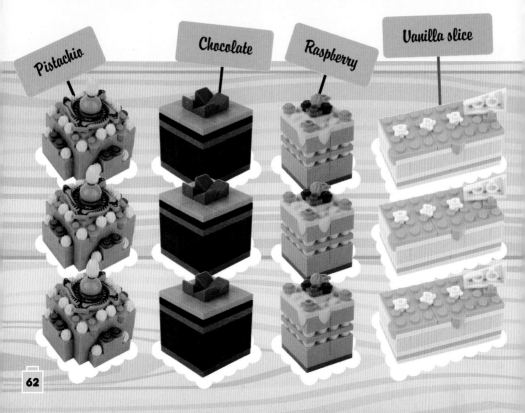

Pistachio

Chocolate

Raspberry

Vanilla slice

STOHRER IS THOUGHT TO BE THE OLDEST PÂTISSERIE IN PARIS HAVING BEEN FOUNDED IN 1730. IT IS LOCATED AT 51 RUE MONTORGUEIL.

BEST PÂTISSERIES IN PARIS

Sample some of the very best pâtisserie that Paris has to offer at these well-known places.

- Pierre Hermé (72 rue Bonaparte)
- Jacques Genin (133 rue de Turenne)
- Jean-Paul Hévin (231 rue Saint-Honoré)
- La Pâtisserie des Rêves (111 rue de Longchamp)
- Ladurée (21 rue Bonaparte)
- Odette (77 rue Galande)

Macaron

Black forest

Opera

TURN OVER TO MAKE

MACARONS

These delicate meringue pâtisserie have been around since the 8th century AD, beginning life as a sort of meringue cookie. They have changed over time to what we now know as two meringue discs filled with a layer of buttercream or ganache.

The exact origins of the macaron in this form are often disputed, but it is widely thought that Pierre Desfontaines, of the Parisian pâtisserie Ladurée is to be thanked for this wonderful creation.

The Ladurée pâtisserie first opened in 1862

THE FIRST LADURÉE MACARON WAS MADE IN PARIS IN 1930 BY LADURÉE'S GRANDSON, PIERRE DESFONTAINES.

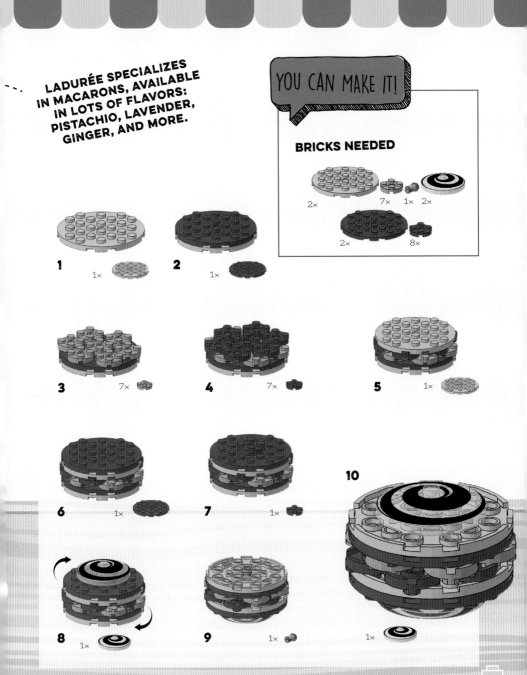

LADURÉE SPECIALIZES IN MACARONS, AVAILABLE IN LOTS OF FLAVORS: PISTACHIO, LAVENDER, GINGER, AND MORE.

YOU CAN MAKE IT!

BRICKS NEEDED

2× 7× 1× 2× 2× 8×

1 1×
2 1×
3 7×
4 7×
5 1×
6 1×
7 1×
8 1×
9 1×
10 1×

BLACK FOREST GATEAU

Try your hand at making this pâtisserie classic—a fun LEGO® version of the chocolate sponge combined with whipped cream and cherries and all finished with a cherry on top.

FRENCH GÂTEAUX USUALLY HAVE SEVERAL LAYERS MADE UP OF THIN SPONGE CAKE AND MOUSSE, GANACHE, OR FRUIT FILLING.

YOU CAN MAKE IT!

BRICKS NEEDED

9× 3× 3×
1× 10× 3×
2× 4×
14× 10× 1× 1×
2× 2× 1× 7×
3× 1× 2× 21×
14× 1× 36×
2× 3× 1× 11×
2× 2× 4× 5×

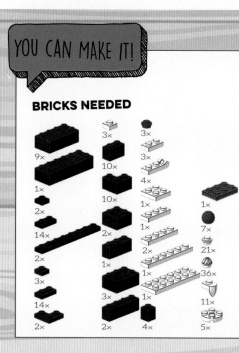

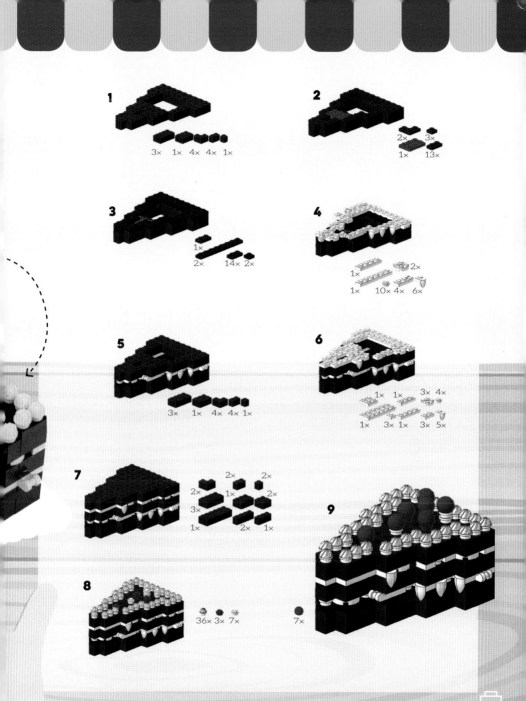

1
3× 1× 4× 4× 1×

2
2× 3×
1× 13×

3
1×
2× 14× 2×

4
1× 2×
1× 10× 4× 6×

5
3× 1× 4× 4× 1×

6
1× 1× 3× 4×
1× 3× 1× 3× 5×

7
2× 2×
2× 1× 2×
3×
1× 2× 1×

8
36× 3× 7×

9
7×

MILLEFEUILLE

This decadent French dessert is made up of crumbly layers of pastry, combined with vanilla pastry cream. Millefeuille is also commonly known as vanilla slice, custard slice, or Napolean.

THE FIRST MENTION OF MILLEFEUILLE DATES BACK TO THE 1600S IN FRANCE.

MILLEFEUILLE TRANSLATES AS "A THOUSAND LEAVES" AND REFERS TO THE INCREDIBLY THIN LAYERS OF PASTRY THAT MAKE UP THE DESSERT.

YOU CAN MAKE IT!

BRICKS NEEDED

2×   1×   4×   1×

4×   2×   4×   2×   3×   3×

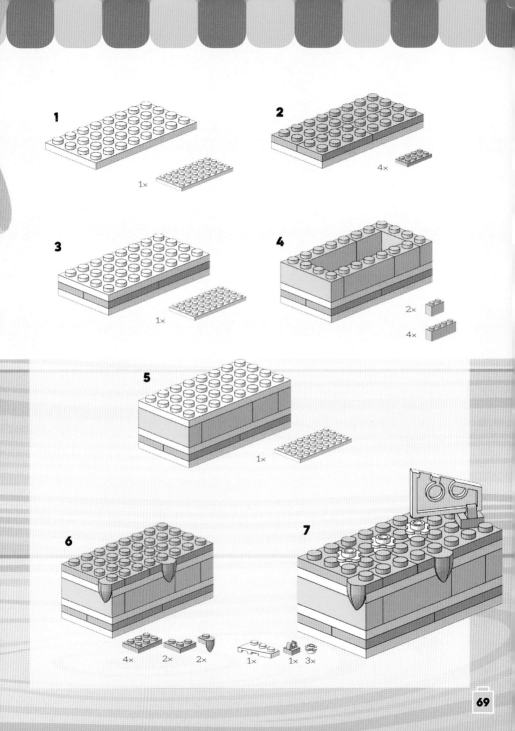

Boulangeries

Paris has roughly 1,200 *boulangeries* (bakeries). Their windows display huge heaps of croissants, baguettes, chocolate éclairs, quiches, pastries, and cakes.

Few things are as tempting as the smell of just-baked buttery croissants wafting out of a bakery. These puffy, crescent-shape pastries are delicious topped with fresh butter, although the French prefer jam or a dip into their coffee.

BOULANGERIES ARE THE PERFECT PLACE FOR A CHEAP LUNCH.

There are so many boulangeries in Paris

Croissant

French people are very fond of this tasty, flaky pastry.

BRICKS NEEDED

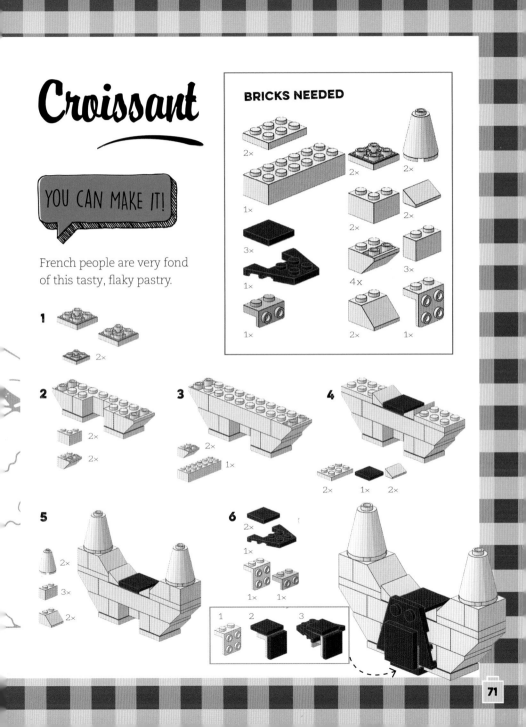

Fromageries

French president Charles de Gaulle once famously asked how it was possible to govern a country with 246 types of cheese. A more relevant question for non-Frenchies: how do you get to grips with a shop that sells such a head-spinning variety? The choices on offer at a Parisian *fromagerie* (cheese shop) can be overwhelming, but the shopkeepers always allow you to try before you buy.

CAUSING A STINK

Fromageries specialize in cheese: whether you want to buy something hard, creamy or moldy, this is the place to go. Expert cheese shop Fromagerie Alléosse is famed for stocking Époisses de Bourgogne—one of the stinkiest! Époisses is left to mature for several weeks (getting smellier by the day), before it's eaten...with a spoon. It's actually banned on public transport!

YOU MIGHT WANT TO BRING YOUR OWN NOSE PEG IF YOU'RE VISITING A FRENCH CHEESE SHOP!

A selection of cheese

CAFÉS

Paris is famed for its café culture. Open from dawn until long after dark, customers park themselves on wicker-chair-lined terraces to see and be seen.

Drinking in Paris essentially means paying the rent for the space you take up so you'll need to come armed with plenty of money. It costs more sitting at tables than standing at the counter, more for prime terrace seats, more on a fancy square than a backstreet, more in fancy neighborhoods, and also more after 10pm, when many places apply a pricier *tarif de nuit* (or night rate).

DRINK YOUR COFFEE AT THE COUNTER FOR A CHEAPER RATE.

TAKE YOUR CAT WITH YOU TO LE CAFÉ DES CHATS!

LE CAFÉ DES CHATS

In the Disney film *The Aristocats*, a butler discovers his rich mistress wants to leave all her money to her cats, so he kidnaps them and they have to find their way back to Paris. The residents of Le Café des Chats would appreciate the story. They're all strays that have been adopted. Customers can enjoy a drink and the company of the furry felines.

COFFEE MACHINE

CREATE SOME SOUND EFFECTS TO GO WITH YOUR TINY COFFEE MACHINE.

French coffee is often regarded as pretty lousy compared with the quality of its cafés, but a new generation of Parisian baristas is changing that and reintroducing the city to freshly roasted beans.

There are more than 9,000 cafés in the city with an open terrace for sitting, sipping, reading, and watching Parisians go by.

COFFEE DECODED

Un café—Single shot of strong espresso.

Un café allongé—Espresso with hot water.

Un café au lait— Coffee with milk.

Un café crème—Shot of espresso with steamed milk.

Un double—Double shot of espresso.

Une noisette—Shot of espresso with a spot of milk.

YOU CAN MAKE IT!

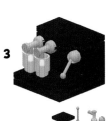
This coffee machine model is cute as a button. All you need to add is the beans!

1

1×

2

4×   2×

3

2×   1×   2×   1×

4

2×   2×

5

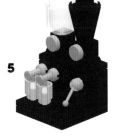

1×   1×   2×

6

3×

ESPRESSO CUP

Build this little coffee cup and set up a fun café in your own home.

DRINK YOUR COFFEE AT THE COUNTER FOR THE CHEAPEST RATE

YOU CAN MAKE IT!

BRICKS NEEDED

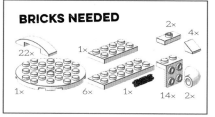

22× 1× 2× 4× 1× 6× 1× 14× 2×

1

1×

2

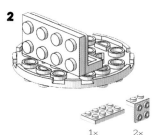

1× 2×

3

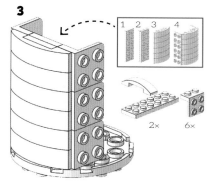

1 2 3 4

2× 6×

4

5

6 4× 2×

7 1×

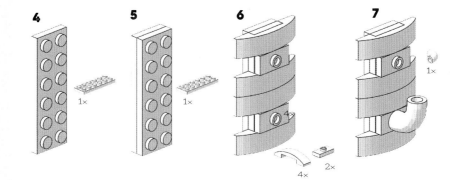

8 1×

9 1×

10 6×

11 6×

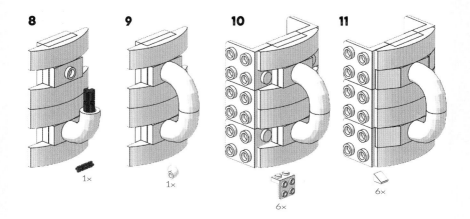

12

13 1 2 ×2 12× 2×

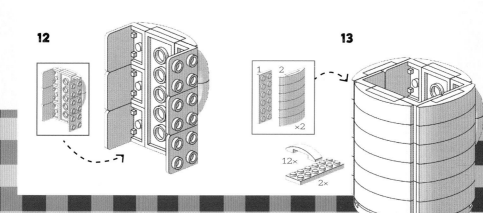

Centre Pompidou

Renowned for its radical architecture, the Centre Pompidou is filled with galleries, cutting-edge exhibitions, and cinemas. France's national collection of art dating from 1905 onward, is the main attraction. A fraction of its 100,000-plus pieces is on display. Nowadays, this quirky arts venue attracts up 25,000 visitors in a single day!

When it opened in 1977 people thought the Centre looked Pompidou more like an oil refinery than an arts centre! Named after former French President Georges Pompidou, the architects effectively designed the building inside out, with plumbing, pipes, air vents, and electrical cables all on the outside!

ADMISSION IS FREE ON THE FIRST SUNDAY OF EACH MONTH.

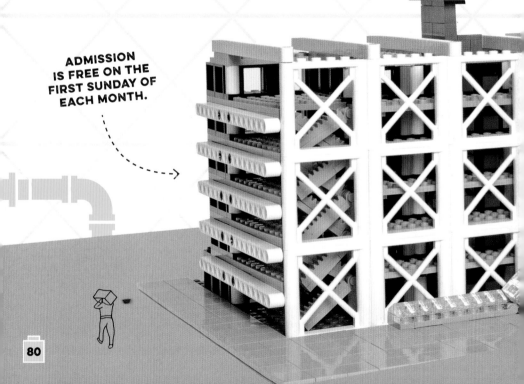

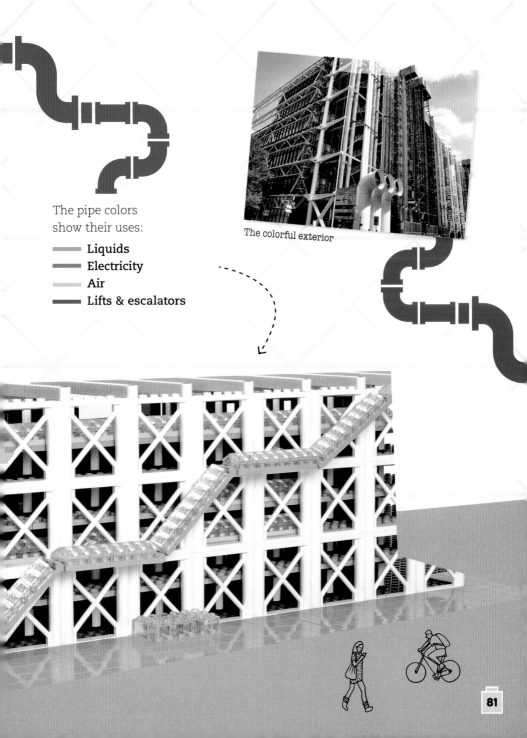

The pipe colors
show their uses:

- Liquids
- Electricity
- Air
- Lifts & escalators

The colorful exterior

The Pompidou's inside-out design is particularly clever as it completely frees up all of the space inside the building. One of its most exciting features is the outside escalator, which snakes up the front of the building in a transparent tunnel. It takes visitors up to the Pompidou's roof, which has amazing panoramic views of the city.

Crazy fountains outside the Pompidou

The colorful statues in the fountains

What's outside?

There are all sorts of exciting things going on outside the Centre Pompidou apart from it's crazy-colored pipe work. The streets nearby are filled with buskers, musicians, jugglers, and mime artists. Place Igor Stravinsky has fairy-tale mechanical fountains, with skeletons, hearts, treble clefs, and even a big pair of ruby-red lips.

Jardin du Luxembourg

When they need a break from all the hustle and bustle, Parisians escape to their elegant parks and tree-lined squares. The city's most popular park is the Jardin du Luxembourg.

Kids laugh at puppet shows and use sticks to chase wooden toy boats around the pond. Old men play quick-fire chess at equally old tables. Office workers catch some sunshine, relaxing in green metal chairs. Musicians strike up at the bandstand. And friends meet and make plans to meet again.

Toy boat

This tiny boat is a fun and easy project to make.

BRICKS NEEDED

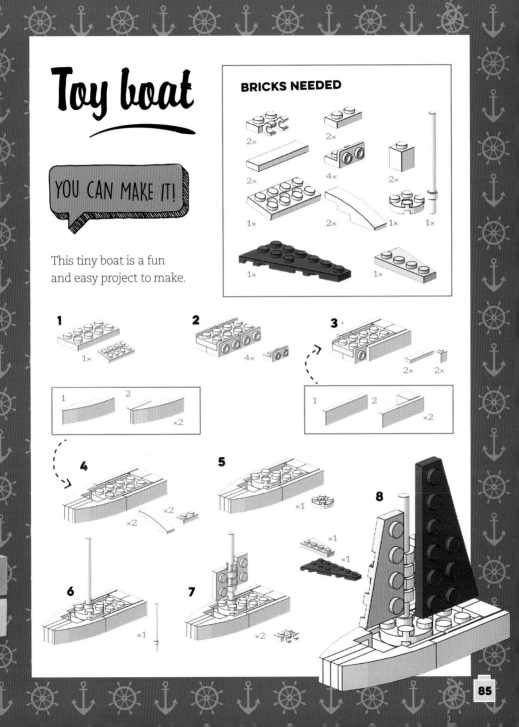

2× 2× 2× 4× 2× 1× 2× 1× 1× 1× 1×

1 1×

2 4×

3 2× 2×

1 2 ×2

1 2 ×2

4 ×2 ×2 ×2

5 ×1

6 ×1

7 ×2

8 ×1 ×1

MONTMARTRE

Hilly Monmartre is a charming Paris neighborhood that has attracted many bohemians and artists to its street over the years. Nowadays this often takes the form of street artists who gather in the lively squares to paint landscapes and sketch; the quality can vary a lot!

Pablo Picasso (1881–1973) was Spanish, but he came to France at the age of 19, barely able to speak a word of French. He moved to Montmartre in 1904 and lived in a filthy studio, with hardly any furniture and paint spattered everywhere. His girlfriend found a mouse in one of his drawers! Picasso's apartment was in a building nicknamed the Laundry Boat, because it creaked and wobbled in the wind, like a laundry boat on the River Seine. It was a great meeting place for artists.

Montmartre is famed for its caricature artists

CUBIST CREATIONS

After Picasso and his friend Georges Braque studied African masks in a Paris museum, they began to experiment with their art. Instead of copying what they could see, they showed their subjects in geometric shapes and from different angles at the same time. This was the beginning of a style of art called cubism.

INDEPENDENCE

Montmartre was considered a separate town to Paris until 1860. The *Montmartrois* (people of Montmartre) still consider themselves to be unofficially separate to the rest of Paris.

PARISIAN ARTISTS

Artists love Paris, and loads of them settled here around the end of the 19th century. They were trying out all kinds of daring new techniques...often leaving critics and the public in shock!

ROOM WITH A VIEW

Camille Pissarro mainly painted countryside scenes, but in the last ten years of his life he had to stay indoors because of an eye infection. He would set himself up in a top-storey Paris hotel room and paint a bird's-eye view of the streets below. In 2014, his painting Le Boulevard Montmartre, Matinée de Printemps (Spring Morning) sold at auction for €26.8 million ($19.7 million).

PARIS'S MONET MUSEUM HAS THE WORLD'S LARGEST COLLECTION OF HIS WATER LILIES PAINTINGS.

LAUTREC IN NUMBERS

Artist Henri de Toulouse-Lautrec was just 36 when he died, but he'd produced:

737 canvases

275 watercolors

353 prints and posters

5,048 drawings

TURN OVER TO MAKE

PAINT PALETTE

CLAUDE MONET
WAS BORN IN PARIS
IN 1840.

Make like Monet with
this model paint palette.
He mixed his hues from
nine different colors.

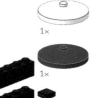

YOU CAN MAKE IT!

BRICKS NEEDED

1×
3×
5×
2×
5×
3×
4×
4×
3×
7×
1×
2×
5×
4×
10×
2×
1×

4×
4×
13×
9×
13×
14×
2×
5×

10×

2×

1×
1×
1×
1×
1×
2×
2×

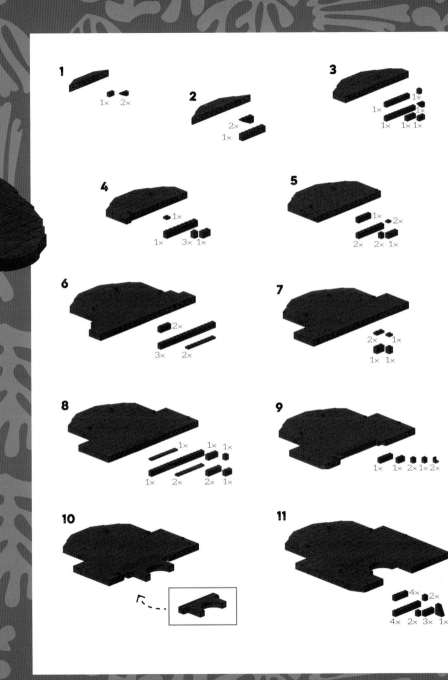

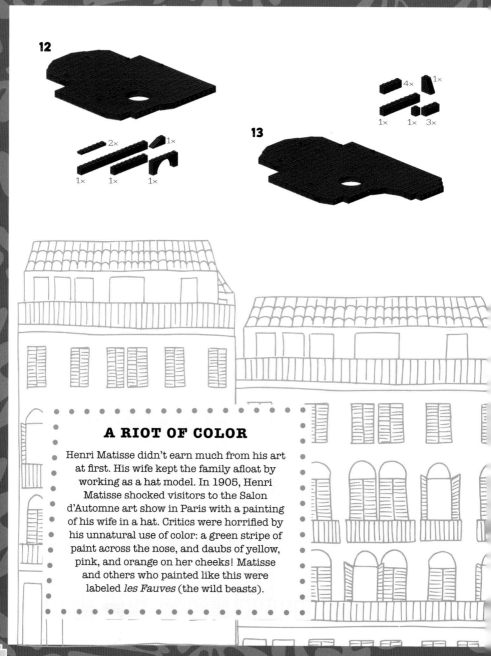

12

4×   1×

1×   1×   3×

2×   1×

1×   1×   1×

13

A RIOT OF COLOR

Henri Matisse didn't earn much from his art
at first. His wife kept the family afloat by
working as a hat model. In 1905, Henri
Matisse shocked visitors to the Salon
d'Automne art show in Paris with a painting
of his wife in a hat. Critics were horrified by
his unnatural use of color: a green stripe of
paint across the nose, and daubs of yellow,
pink, and orange on her cheeks! Matisse
and others who painted like this were
labeled *les Fauves* (the wild beasts).

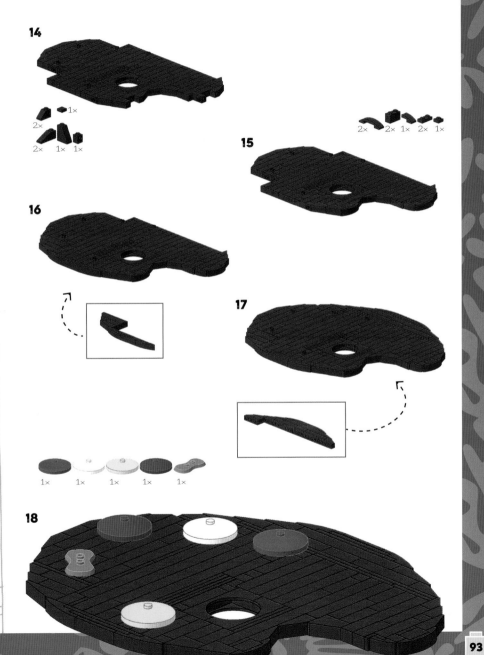

14

1×
2×
2× 1× 1×

2× 2× 1× 2× 1×

15

16

17

1× 1× 1× 1× 1×

18

Mona Lisa

The star of the show at the Louvre is the mysterious Mona Lisa, painted by Italian artist Leonardo da Vinci in the 16th century; King Francis I of France bought it to hang in his bathroom.

This might be the world's most famous painting, but in 1911 hardly anyone had heard of it. In August of that year, a workman at the Louvre hid overnight in a cupboard, slipped the painting from its frame, and left with it under his jacket. A huge hunt ensued—it took 27 months to recover.

Mother Mona

For centuries admirers have wondered about the Mona Lisa. Is she mourning the death of a loved one or in love with her painter? Scientists used infrared technology to peer through paint layers and confirm Mona Lisa's identity as Lisa Gherardini, wife of a merchant from Florence. They discovered her dress was covered in a transparent veil usually worn by pregnant women or new mothers. They think that the work was painted to celebrate the birth of her second son around 1503, when she was aged about 24.

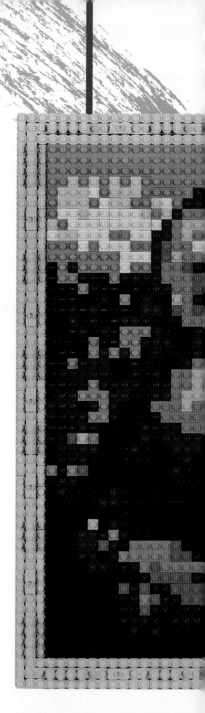

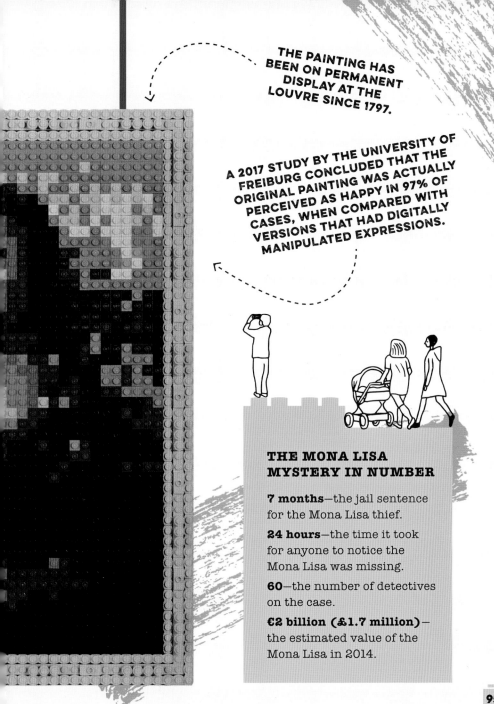

THE PAINTING HAS BEEN ON PERMANENT DISPLAY AT THE LOUVRE SINCE 1797.

A 2017 STUDY BY THE UNIVERSITY OF FREIBURG CONCLUDED THAT THE ORIGINAL PAINTING WAS ACTUALLY PERCEIVED AS HAPPY IN 97% OF CASES, WHEN COMPARED WITH VERSIONS THAT HAD DIGITALLY MANIPULATED EXPRESSIONS.

THE MONA LISA MYSTERY IN NUMBER

7 months—the jail sentence for the Mona Lisa thief.

24 hours—the time it took for anyone to notice the Mona Lisa was missing.

60—the number of detectives on the case.

€2 billion (£1.7 million)—the estimated value of the Mona Lisa in 2014.

SACRÉ-COEUR

More than just a place of worship, visiting the dove-white *Basilique du Sacré-Cœur* (Sacred Heart Basilica) is a real experience. It wasn't until 1919 that Sacré-Cœur was declared sacred, in contrast to the surrounding area's bohemian residents. It is reached via 270 steps, which give a postcard-perfect city panorama. Buskers and street artists perform here while picnickers spread out on the hillside park.

The basilica's white stone gives off a mineral that means it stays white despite weathering and pollution.

LOTS OF VISITORS

Sacré-Coeur attracts more than 11.5 million visitors each year, making it the most visited church after Notre-Dame cathedral (see page 48).

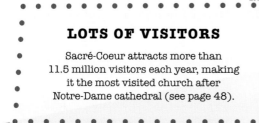

THERE ARE 270 STEPS UP TO SACRÉ-COEUR.

ON TOP OF THE WORLD

The church's dome is the second highest point in Paris after the Eiffel Tower! The whole building sits on top of Montmartre—originally known as the Mount of Mars, and a pagan site of worship.

TURN OVER TO MAKE

YOU CAN MAKE IT!

Hold Sacré-Cœur in the palm of your hand with this build, which uses some interesting bricks.

The beautiful Sacré-Coeur

THERE ARE NAMES OF ANYONE WHO DONATED MONEY TOWARD THE CONSTRUCTION ENGRAVED ALL OVER THE WALLS OF THE CHURCH.

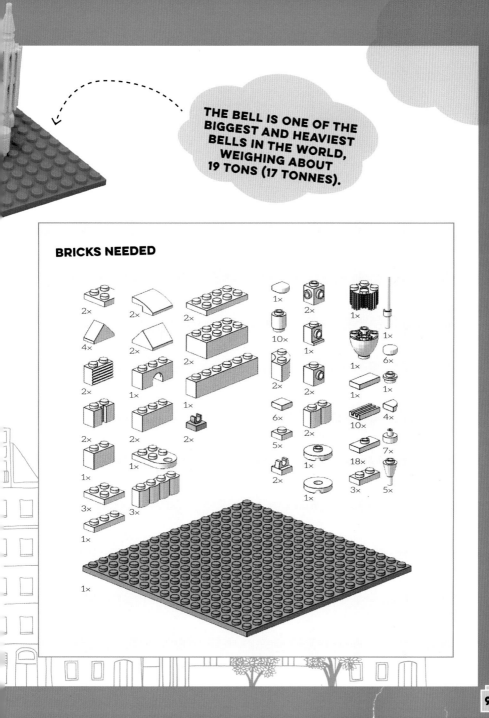

THE BELL IS ONE OF THE BIGGEST AND HEAVIEST BELLS IN THE WORLD, WEIGHING ABOUT 19 TONS (17 TONNES).

BRICKS NEEDED

2×
2×
2×

4×
2×
2×

2×
1×
2×

1×

2×
2×
2×

2×
1×
1×

3×
3×

1×

1×

1×
10×
2×
1×
6×
5×

2×

2×
1×
2×
2×
2×
1×

1×

2×
1×
1×
6×
10×
4×
18×
7×
3×
5×

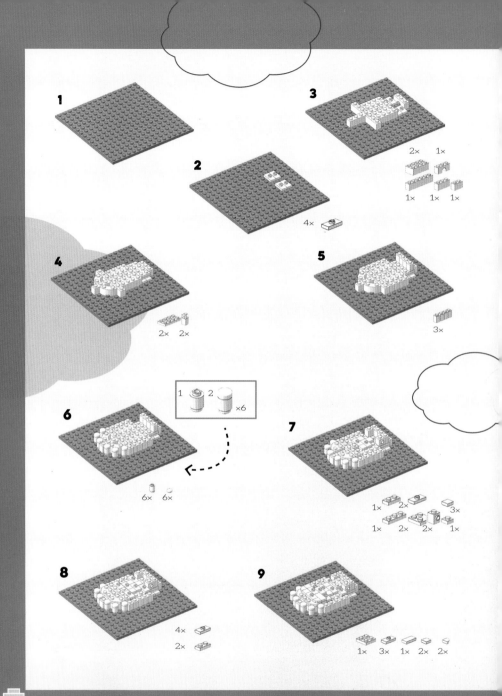

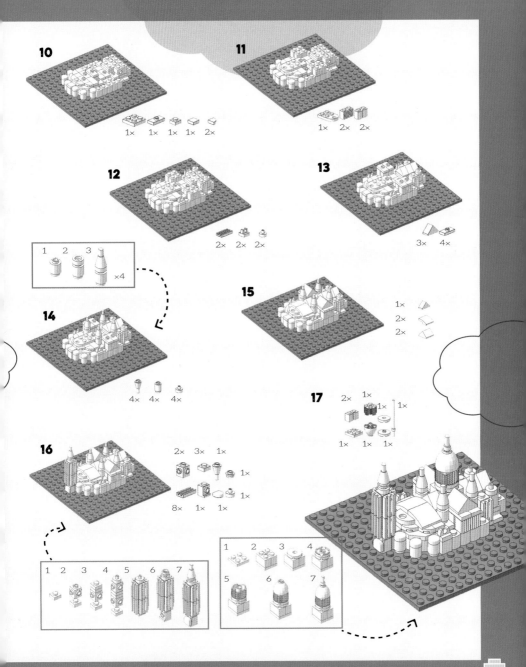

10

1× 1× 1× 1× 2×

11

1× 2× 2×

12

2× 2× 2×

13

3× 4×

1 2 3

×4

14

4× 4× 4×

15

1×
2×
2×

16

2× 3× 1×

1×

8× 1× 1×

1×

17

2× 1×

1× 1×

1× 1× 1×

1 2 3 4 5 6 7

1 2 3 4

5 6 7

Moulin Rouge

Surprisingly, Paris's most famous windmill never worked at all! The sails of the *Moulin Rouge* (Red Windmill) only turned to draw crowds to the cabaret club beneath it. There, they watched high-kicking girls in swirling skirts dance the can-can. The name "can-can" actually means "scandal." Nineteenth-century Parisians were shocked and scandalized by the dance and some performers were even arrested for showing off too much leg!

Immortalized in painter Henri de Toulouse-Lautrec's posters and later, on film, Paris' legendary cabaret now twinkles beneath a 1925 replica of its original red windmill. From the opening bars of music to the last can-can kick, it's still an exciting whirl of fantastical costumes, dazzling sets, and exhausting-looking choreography.

CLOSED FOR RENOVATION

In 1915 the Moulin Rouge was completely destroyed by a fire. The cabaret had to shut down for six years to be completely rebuilt and opened again in 1921 after the end of WWI.

The Paris landscape was once dotted with over 300 windmills (*moulins*). In the past they were essential for grinding wheat and crushing grapes, but only a few remain. The *Moulin de la Galette*, in Montmartre, is nearly 500 years old and stopped working years ago.

The Moulin Rouge windmill is a city icon

MUSÉE DES ARTS ET MÉTIERS

Paris's *Musée des Arts et Métiers* (or Arts and Crafts Museum) is devoted to science and invention; it's full of amazing machines, cars, planes, and all kinds of weird and wonderful contraptions.

One of its most famous exhibits was the pendulum created by Léon Foucault in 1851, to prove to Napoleon III that the earth rotates on its axis each day. The pendulum swung from the museum roof from 1855, until it suddenly smashed to the ground in 2010. Luckily, there's still a working replica of the original model in the Panthéon in Paris.

Maritime metro station

In the 19th century, French author Jules Verne wrote worldwide bestsellers that seemed to predict the future. Nautilus, the submarine he imagined in *20,000 Leagues Under the Sea* inspired the decor at the Arts et Métiers metro station.

WHILE DA VINCI'S FLYING MACHINE IS NOT DISPLAYED IN THE MUSÉE DES ARTS ET MÉTIERS, IT UNDOUBTEDLY INSPIRED MANY OF THE MACHINES FEATURED THERE.

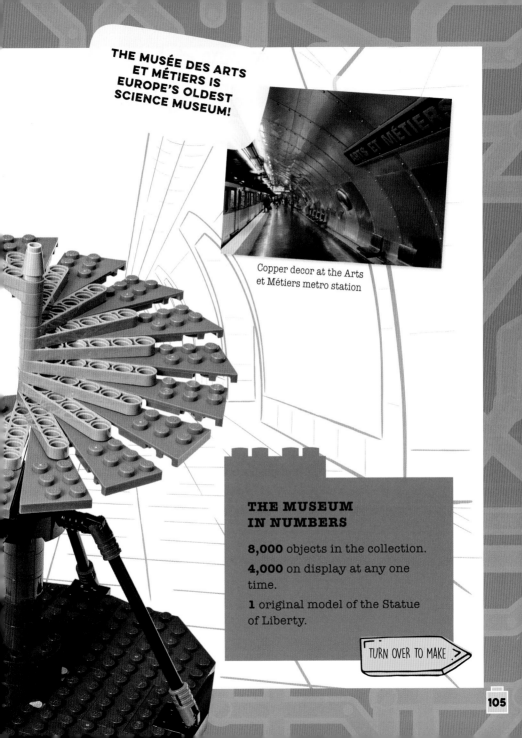

THE MUSÉE DES ARTS ET MÉTIERS IS EUROPE'S OLDEST SCIENCE MUSEUM!

Copper decor at the Arts et Métiers metro station

THE MUSEUM IN NUMBERS

8,000 objects in the collection.

4,000 on display at any one time.

1 original model of the Statue of Liberty.

TURN OVER TO MAKE

FLYING MACHINE

The museum features steam-powered airplanes influenced by the ideas of Leonardo da Vinci. His designs for a flying machine inspired the first helicopters.

A PIONEER!

The first helicopter wasn't built until the 1940s, but it is believed that Leonardo da Vinci's sketches from the late 15th century mapped out how the device could work.

YOU CAN MAKE IT!

BRICKS NEEDED

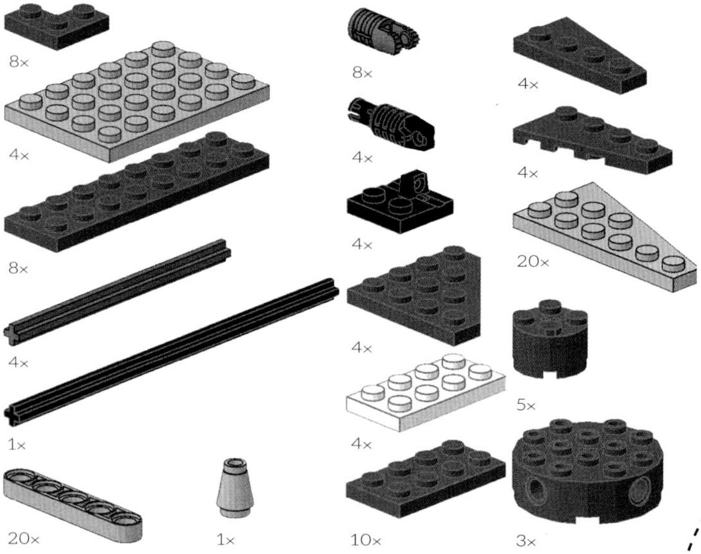

8×

4×

8×

4×

20×

1×

8×

4×

4×

4×

5×

4×

10×

3×

4×

1×

1

2

4×
4×
4×
4×

3

8×
10×
4×

4×
4×

4

2× 5×

5

1× 4×

6

4× 8×

×20

7

1×

8

9

1×

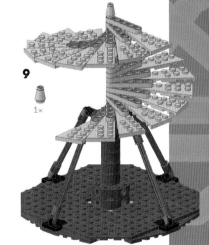

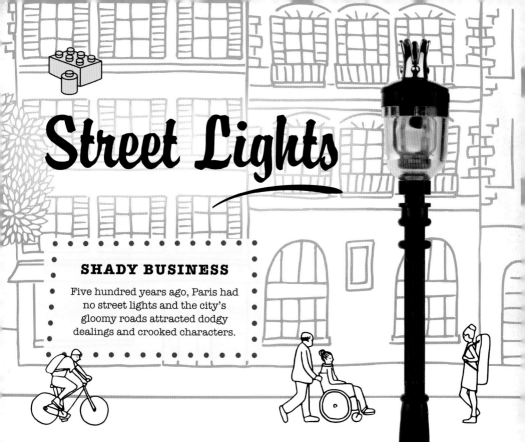

Street Lights

Nicknamed the "City of Lights," Paris got its
illuminating name because the city started
Europe's Age of Enlightenment in the 18th century.
The city has thousands of street lights and many
of them have peered over the city for years. They
each have their own stories to tell.

During the French Revolution the street lights were
smashed so that revolutionaries could sneak around
in secret. Some street lights were used as gallows to
hang unpopular aristocrats. Street lights are still
revolutionary symbols to this day. The French
saying is *à la lanterne!*—or "string 'em up!"

YOU CAN MAKE IT!

This model is one of Paris's famous candelabra street lights, which can be found by the famous steps of Montmartre. Its distinctive feature is the crown on top.

BRICKS NEEDED

8×

1×

1×

1×

1×

1×

1×

1×

1×

1×

1×

1×

1×

1×

1×

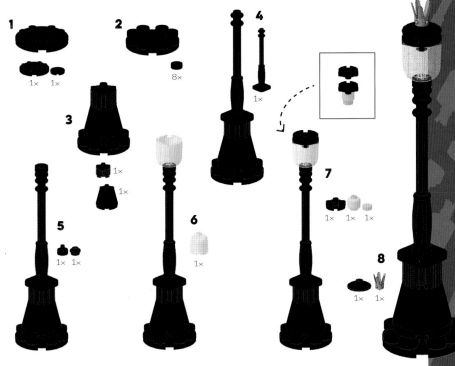

1
1× 1×

2
8×

3
1×
1×

4
1×

5
1× 1×

6
1×

7
1× 1× 1×

8
1× 1×

Les Catacombes

Sixty six feet (20m) below ground, in the limestone tunnels that sprawl beneath Paris, lie the skeletons of six to seven million Parisians. The public can explore 1.24 miles (2km) of the tunnels, but that's just a fraction of the 186 miles (300km) that actually exist. Tickets for tomb tours are hard to get hold of, and most of the tunnels are strict no-go zones, but that doesn't stop people sneaking down to take a peek.

Skeletons were moved to the catacombs in 1786, when Paris cemeteries became seriously overcrowded. It took two years to transfer them from just one of the cemeteries—workers brought in piles of bones by wheelbarrow. Famous people and victims of the Revolution are buried here, including some who had been guillotined.

DODGE THE CATA-COPS

Under cover of darkness, cataphiles open up secret entrances and creep into the catacombs—through a manhole cover or basement car park, perhaps. They explore using maps and might even host a dinner party down there! In 2004, the cataflics even found a secret cinema down there!

THE CATACOMB WALLS ARE LINED WITH BONES.

The eerie walls of the catacombes

CATACOMB LINGO

Cataphiles—people who dodge the cata-cops.

Cataflics—the police whose job it is to keep them out!

THE TEMPERATURE IN THE TUNNELS STAYS A STEADY 57°F (14°C) ALL YEAR ROUND.

TURN OVER TO MAKE

Skull

There are three times more dead Parisians lying beneath Paris sidewalks than live ones walking around on them today! What will you call your friendly model skull?

YOU CAN MAKE IT!

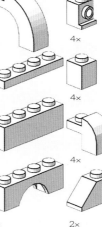

BRICKS NEEDED

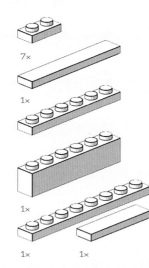

7×

1×

1×

1×

1×

4×

2×

2×

4×

4×

4×

4×

2×

2×

2×

4×

4×

2×

2×

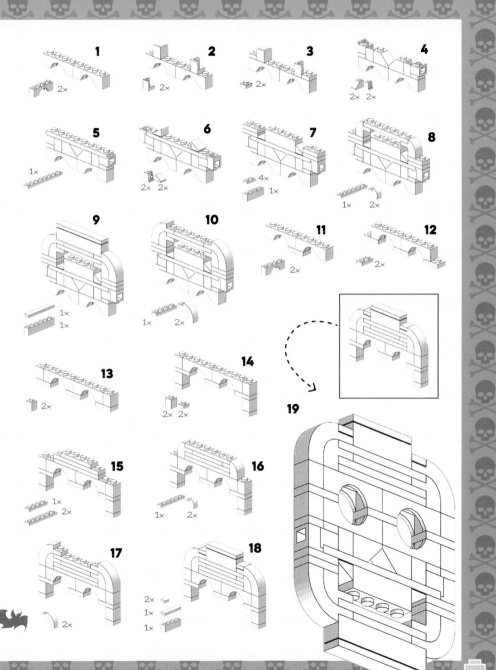

PÈRE LACHAISE CEMETERY

The world's most visited cemetery, Père Lachaise, opened in Paris in 1804. It is as big as 30 soccer fields and contains more than 70,000 graves. The "streets" are lined with trees and tiny buildings with front doors that hide tombs behind them. Lots are eerily beautiful, decorated with carvings. Actors, composers, painters, writers, singers...all kinds of people are buried here, many of them superstars of their day.

Irish writer and poet Oscar Wilde is buried here. Fans traditionally touched up their lipstick then puckered up their lips and left a lip print on his tomb, which was designed by sculptor Sir Jacob Epstein and shaped like a winged messenger. When the authorities put glass walls around it, the fans began kissing the glass instead!

GHOSTLY APPARITIONS

This cemetery is said to be one of the most haunted places in the world. A shadowy Jim Morrison has been spied wandering near his own grave, and get too close to the grave of ex-Prime Minister Adolphe Thiers and his ghost may tug at your clothes...yikes!

Oscar Wilde's tomb

PÈRE LACHAISE
IN NUMBERS

109 acres (44 hectares)

70,000 tombs

800,000 people buried here

2 million annual visitors

Jim Morrison's grave

TOP OF THE TOMBS

The most visited grave belongs to
superstar poet and singer-
songwriter Jim Morrison, who died
mysteriously in a Paris hotel bath at
the age of just 27. Fans still visit
every day; some leave poems and
messages, others graffiti and
cigarette butts. Over 40 years later,
Jim's death is still a mystery. One
theory says the grave is empty and
the death was just a hoax.

A cunning PR plan

When Père Lachaise cemetery opened, in 1804, no one wanted to be buried here. At the start it had only 13 graves! So, the administrators staged a clever publicity stunt. They brought in the bodies of dead celebrities—the playwright Molière and legendary lovers Abelard and Heloise—and reburied them on the new site. The plan worked, and by 1830, the grave count had reached 33,000.

TREES GALORE

According to latest figures there are over 4,000 trees on the site of the cemetery. Species of trees include maple, chestnut, ash, cedar, walnut, beechwood, and others.

Château de Versailles

It's probably the most famous palace in the world, but back in 1682, the Château de Versailles, a short train (RER) ride away from Paris, was just a humble hunting lodge. France's King Louis XIV (known as the "Sun King") transformed it, adding wings to turn it into a palace, and new buildings and gardens. Thirty thousand workers and soldiers built the palace with all the most beautiful and expensive materials, with an eye-watering price tag to match. Louis then moved his government here with 6,000 courtiers!

The palace and gardens of Versailles are laid out in such a way that, when seen from above, they have a symmetrical beauty. The landscape architect for the project had to flatten hills, drain marshes, and relocate forests to make room for the endless gardens, ponds, and fountains.

THE ROYAL MENAGERIE

In the 18th century it was normal for royals to keep exotic pets. At the time of Louis XVI, the private Versailles menagerie included: a lion, a panther, a tiger, hyenas, and monkeys.

Versaille's impressive gardens

CHANDELIER

King Louis XIV kept adding extras to Versailles, including a spectacular Hall of Mirrors (or *Galerie des Glaces*), a 256-foot- (75m-) long ballroom, and a 4,921-foot- (1,500m-) long canal in the garden, with real gondola boats shipped in from Venice!

The Hall of Mirrors is Versailles' opulent central room, featuring 357 of the shiny things, and many huge, twinkling chandeliers. You can make your own, at a fraction of the cost!

YOU CAN MAKE IT!

BRICKS NEEDED

16×

2×

16×

134×

16×

1×

12×

16×

16×

1×

2×

16×

1×

8×

1×

16×

4×

ON CEREMONY

The king was on display at all times. One hundred courtiers watched him wash and dress in his bedroom; he even had a ceremony for taking off his boots!

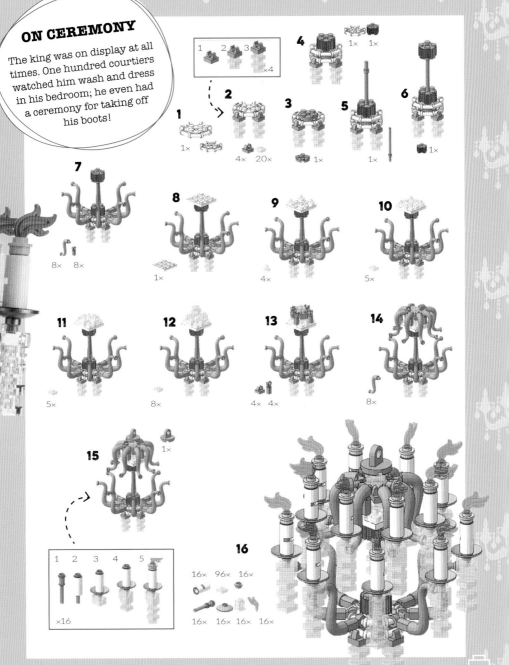

Metro

A whole different city, filled with underground tunnels, canals, sewers, crypts, and cellars, rumbles on under Parisians' feet. Trains trundle along the tracks of the metro for 19 hours a day—it's one of the world's busiest underground railways.

Palais-Royal— Musée du Louvre

Welcome to the zaniest station entrance in Paris. Called the Kiosk of the Nightwalkers, it has two giant, sparkly crowns hovering over the stairs. Each is made of aluminum poles threaded with 800 colored glass baubles.

Palais-Royal—Musée du Louvre

THE SOUND OF MUSIC

Paris's underground stations are filled with music! Live performance is so important to travelers, the metro even employs its own artistic director. Each year thousands of musicians audition for 300 prized spots in the city's underground. Licensed performers are allowed to play in the long corridors, but not on train platforms.

THE AVERAGE JOURNEY TIME BETWEEN PARIS METRO STATIONS IS A MERE MINUTE!

THE METRO IN NUMBERS

1.5 billion annual passengers.

303 stations

600,000 miles (965,606km) traveled by the trains each day on the **132 miles (212km)** of track (like going right round the world **24** times!)

ABBESSES

At 118 feet (36m) below ground, Abbesses station is the deepest, and also one of the most beautiful, metro stations in Paris. Its entrance is probably the most photographed too, boasting the fancy art-nouveau style that was hip 100 years ago.

10 most useful bricks

These are the most exciting bricks in LEGO® building. No matter how many of them you have, there will never quite be enough!

1

2×4 BRICK

The oldest brick around, this is a classic. Strong, and great for adding structure to something fragile.

2

1×2 BRACKET

Introduced in 2012, and so useful! These pieces help where other brackets can't and add real strength to your models.

3

1×1×⅔ SLOPE
(or "cheese" slope)

A great piece that gives models a smooth, modern look. Useful for buildings, vehicles and animals.

4

1×1 ROUND PLATE WITH HOLE

These parts are perfect for anchoring rods.

5

TECHNIC PIN JOINER

Structural steelwork is very important in architecture and these pieces joined together are just the right shape.

6

1×4 PLATE HINGE

Small but strong hinges that let you choose the exact angle for the pieces of your creation.

SOME REALLY USEFUL TIPS

BUILD TIPS

BRICKS AND PLATES

One LEGO® brick is equal in height to three LEGO® plates. Plates give models more strength (they make great floors), and can incorporate more color variety and detail in the same space as a brick (see below).

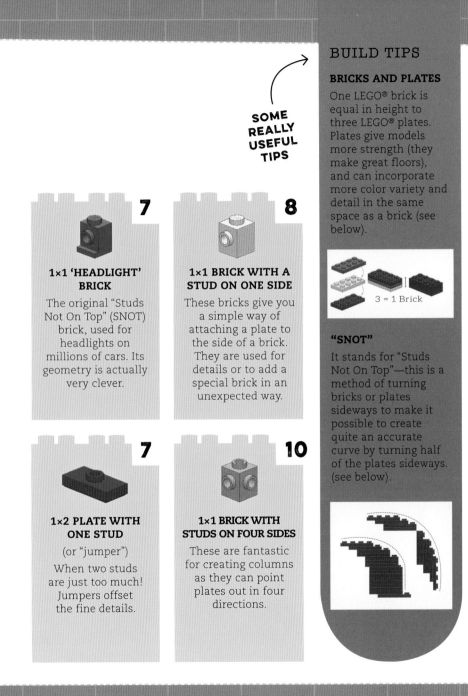

3 = 1 Brick

"SNOT"

It stands for "Studs Not On Top"—this is a method of turning bricks or plates sideways to make it possible to create quite an accurate curve by turning half of the plates sideways. (see below).

7

1×1 'HEADLIGHT' BRICK

The original "Studs Not On Top" (SNOT) brick, used for headlights on millions of cars. Its geometry is actually very clever.

8

1×1 BRICK WITH A STUD ON ONE SIDE

These bricks give you a simple way of attaching a plate to the side of a brick. They are used for details or to add a special brick in an unexpected way.

7

1×2 PLATE WITH ONE STUD

(or "jumper")
When two studs are just too much! Jumpers offset the fine details.

10

1×1 BRICK WITH STUDS ON FOUR SIDES

These are fantastic for creating columns as they can point plates out in four directions.

LEGO® colors

With more than 140 LEGO® colors to choose from, which should you use?

Not all parts exist in all colors, and in fact some very common parts have never been made in some of the obvious colors.

Below and opposite is a guide to some, but not all, of the colors available, using their Bricklink names rather than the official LEGO® ones.

HOW TO FIND THE BRICKS YOU'LL NEED

No matter how many LEGO® bricks anyone has—it's never enough! You don't need to worry if you don't have exactly the same bricks as I've used for these models though. Just try building them with the bricks you have and your imagination!

If you do need to buy more bricks to build some of the models in this book, then I've got some tips for you. Did you know you can buy bricks directly from www.LEGO.com? There is a special section on their online store, just for bricks. Here you can choose from a huge selection of bricks in all sorts of colors to help you build your city. If you're after something very special though, there are special websites allowing people like you to trade bricks? The two best known are www.bricklink.com and www.brickowl.com.

DARK PURPLE

TAN

TRANS-NEON ORANGE

TRANS-PINK

LIGHT YELLOW

DARK BROWN

PINK

TRANS-BLUE

TRANS-GREEN

OLIVE GREEN

PEARL GOLD

TRANS-LIGHT BLUE

CHROME SILVER

BRIGHT LIGHT BLUE

DARK FLESH

LIGHT PURPLE

AQUA

**FUN RANGE
OF COLORS**

TURQUOISE	SAND BLUE	PEARL LIGHT GRAY	PEARL BLACK	BRIGHT YELLOW	TRANS-RED

YELLOW	EARTH ORANGE	VIOLET	DARK RED	TRANS-PURPLE	TRANS-NEON GREEN

SAND GREEN	TRANS-DARK BLUE	TRANS-ORANGE	BRIGHT PINK	DARK BLUISH-GRAY	DARK ORANGE

TRANS-CLEAR	REDDISH BROWN	DARK TURQUOISE	TRANS-BLACK	DARK PINK	RED

PEARL SILVER	WHITE	LIGHT BLUISH-GRAY	GREEN	DARK AZURE	DARK TAN

PURPLE	MARBLED SILVER	ORANGE	MEDIUM DARK PINK	TRANS-YELLOW	BRIGHT GREEN

BLUE	LIGHT ORANGE	BRIGHT LIGHT YELLOW	DARK GREEN	LIME GREEN

DARK BLUE	MEDIUM BLUE	BLACK	MAERSK BLUE

Acknowledgments

I'd like to thank the other amazing builders who helped to contribute to this book. My thanks to Alastair Disley, Kirsten Bedigan, Guy Bagley, and Teresa Elsmore for being instrumental in bringing the book to life!

WE ALWAYS LIKE TO SAY THANK YOU!

Picture Credits

The publisher would like to thank the following for permission to reproduce copyright material:

Alamy: p30 Eddie Linssen; p32 Rachel Davies; p39 Alexandre Rotenberg; p83 Hercules Milas; p105 Bruce Bi;

Shutterstock: p10 Claudia Carlsen; p21 Leonid Andronov; p26 (top) ansharphoto; p26 (bottom) Stefano Ember; p28, 59 pisaphotography; p35 antoniobarrosfr; p40 DuxX; P43 Dutourdumonde Photography; P50, 54 Bill Perry; p64 cdrin; p70 Gorodisskij; p73 kykykis; p81 Jorge Felix Costa; p82 E.O.; p86 T.W. van Urk; p98 IM_photo; p103 maziarz; p111 observe.co; p114 Jaime Pharr; p116 HUNAG Zheng; p119 Kirill Neiezhmakov; p122 Kiev.Viktor.

LEGO builders: p10 Arc de Triomphe, p12 Place Charles de Gaulle, p1, 9, 15 Scooter, p4, 8, 17 Tour de France Cyclist, p9, 20 Guillotine, p24, 27 Pont Neuf, p8, 28 Padlock, p5, 30 Love Heart, p32, 34 Paris Fashion Week, p37 Shopping in Paris, p38 Perfume Bottle, p9, 40 Poodle, p.46–7 Aquarium, p3, 9, 48–53 Notre-Dame de Paris, p55 Stained Glass, p9, 56 Bell Towers, p62–63 Patisseries, p8, 65 Macarons, p4, 8, 66 Black Forest Gateau, p9, 68 Millefeuille, p1, 8, 71 Croissant, p73 Fromageries, p8, 76 Coffee Machine, p9, 78 Espresso Cup, 80–3 Centre Pompidou, p8, 85 Toy Boat, p86 Montmartre, p8, 88–93 Paint Palette, p94 Mona Lisa, p5, 9, 97–101 Sacré-Coeur, p102 Can-can Dancers, p8, 104–107 Flying Machine, p8, 108 Street Lights, p9, 111–113 Skull, p115–117 Pere Lachaise Cemetery, p119 Chateau de Versailles, p9, 120 Chandelier, p122 Metro Station © Warren Elsmore; p7, 43–5 Eiffel Tower © Spencer Rezkalla; p74 Café © Teresa Elsmore; p58–61 Rooftops © Alastair Sisley.

While every effort has been made to credit photographers, The Bright Press would like to apologize should there have been any omissions or errors, and would be pleased to make the appropriate correction for future editions of the book.

ABOUT THE AUTHOR

Warren Elsmore is an artist in LEGO® bricks and a lifelong fan of LEGO®. He is based in Edinburgh, UK. He has been in love with the little bricks since the age of four and is now heavily involved in the LEGO® fan community. Since rediscovering his love of LEGO® at the age of 24, Warren has never looked back. In 2012, after 15 years in a successful IT career, he moved to working full time with LEGO® bricks and now helps many companies to realise their own dreams in plastic. He is the author of several LEGO® books and has organized several international LEGO® conventions.